THE
ENTREPRENEUR
MINDSET SHIFT

Owning Your Own Global Home Business

For Business Leaders Tired Of The
Corporate Shackles—Ready To Shift
Into Entrepreneurial Freedom

THE ENTREPRENEUR MINDSET SHIFT

Owning Your Own Global Home Business

10 Myths Every Business Leader Needs
To Break Through Before Building
Their Own Business From Home

CLIFF WALKER

The World's #1 Authority On
Building A Global Home Business

Published By: Global Success Systems LLC
Website: www.CliffWalker.com

PRAISE FOR THE AUTHOR

"I am very grateful that the universe finally aligned to let me work together with Cliff. I have been in the home business industry for 10 years and never seen anyone that supports his team like he does. The systems and tools that he gives freely, along with coaching, support and a huge willingness to develop success in others, make Cliff extraordinary in this industry."

Andrew Smith, US

"On meeting Cliff I was refreshingly impressed by his positive, no-hype approach to business. I have found him to be a person of high integrity who provides a collaborative and supportive environment to work within.

Cliff has provided the professional leadership required to help me successfully transition from a corporate background to the network marketing field. He is genuinely passionate about helping others succeed and is a true professional at doing so."

Andrew Price, UK

"Cliff's help and guidance has enabled me as a first timer in network marketing to build a team of tens of thousands of people all around the world and to create a six-figure residual income in under two years, all while working part-time from home and enjoying total time freedom. He is one of the best leaders I've ever seen!"

Ellen Williams, AU

"Since meeting Cliff I have found a new level of mentorship and business knowledge, rarely found amongst professionals. Most provide great and motivational information but few, and maybe only Cliff, give that unique ingredient mix of availability and communication.

No matter where in the world he may be, you can be sure he has time for you and anybody in your team. He demonstrates perfectly that old adage,

'People don't care how much you know until they know how much you care.' Cliff makes sure you know he cares."

James Lamb, Spain

"Cliff is the greatest leader I have ever met in network marketing. His vision and commitment to help others to succeed is incredible. The systems he has created to teach and support his team are absolutely unique and priceless. It was an honour to work with him and an absolutely amazing experience."

Tania Vassileva, Bulgaria

"Having over 30 years of sales experience, I've had the opportunity to be trained and mentored by those who are known to be some of the most influential and successful leaders in network marketing. Cliff, however, is a cut above them all.

He carries a spirit of excellence and compassionately breathes hope and encouragement into you, while also transferring the business and *relationship building skills needed for success—without compromising your values.*

Cliff is a leader who goes above and beyond the call of duty to mentor, guide and cheer you on to your own personal victory. He is able to do this with the utmost integrity, tough love and tenacity. He has the ability to get you super-charged, along with instilling an unstoppable belief within yourself to push for your personal best!"

Lyn Flaherty, US

"Cliff is among the most successful network marketing leaders I've known—and not simply from the measure of how much money he has made.

He is thoughtful and deliberate in his strategies, while being passionate and ensuring their execution. His advocacy for personal development and principle-based living is not only a directive for those he mentors but also a practice he himself embraces.

Cliff's approach, priorities and lifestyle all exemplify an attainable and very real demonstration of what it means to achieve success. He is not just one to follow, but one to model."

Steve Dailey, US

CONTENTS

INTRODUCTION

Y ou are probably reading this book because you are considered a business leader in your organisation who is highly skilled and respected.

You have spent most of your career inside someone else's organisation as an employee, working your way up each rung of the corporate ladder.

Climbing the corporate structure is the model that many follow and stay in for their entire lives.

Of course, they accept everything that comes with that along the way...like corporate politics, not having the freedom they desire and limits to the income they can achieve.

The question you need to ask yourself is: "Am I willing to sacrifice my dreams and desires by remaining in the corporate world, or is it time for me to explore the other world of entrepreneurial freedom?"

If that is the crossroads where you are right now, then this is the book that will finally put you on the right track.

How do I know this?

I spent years and years climbing all of the rungs on that corporate ladder. I have worked for some big companies, including drink giant Diageo, which owns a huge number of brands, including Smirnoff, Guinness and Johnnie Walker.

When I worked for them, I had a great salary, great benefits and great bonuses, but it never felt like freedom and it never felt like it was mine or that I had any ownership over the position.

I was a cog in a machine—a fairly important one, no doubt, but still a cog.

I ticked every box you can think of from a corporate point of view, and I suppose it could be considered the definition of success within that circle. I enjoyed international travel, expense accounts and promotion after promotion. I was hitting targets, impressing each new boss as I moved up, but never felt truly fulfilled.

Traveling on business isn't really traveling because you don't get to see anything. You go from the airport to the hotel and from the hotel to the meeting room. If you are lucky, you get a nice meal at the end of the day.

Then you have to leave, and the company wants you on to the next meeting.

It's the same when you are spending on expense accounts—it isn't really spending. You have to justify everything purchased, and you don't really own what you buy—the company does.

The other issue I had with the corporate world was that, no matter how high up I got, I always seemed to be competing with others. There was always a new boss to impress, and this meant always being ready to play politics and stay on their good side. You have to learn how they work, how to get ahead in their eyes and how to fall in line with their way of thinking.

Sometimes this can be really tough, with a lot of personality clashes that are a real pain in the backside.

To top it all off, no matter how hard I worked or how successful I was, there was always a ceiling on how much I could earn. That was until I came across an alternative that gave me the opportunity to completely change the way I worked, the way I earned an income. More significantly, it gave me the opportunity to change my lifestyle.

I came across this business system as a management consultant. I was being paid rather a lot of money to decipher whether business models could be applied to certain projects and how those scenarios might play out.

While working on a project for a client, I came across the direct to consumer marketing model and, I have to say, it fascinated me. As I thoroughly reviewed the model, I began to see that it was actually a system with a stunning amount of promise, although it had been used and abused by a lot of companies. Over time, it had garnered a reputation which was underserving of the business science that it was based on.

So, with a fresh pair of eyes and my usual analytical tool set, I looked past the anecdotal assumptions and studied the core business acumen that could be applied to the true structure underpinning the system.

It was a eureka moment for me because not only did I truly understand the potential but I also knew how I, with my years of corporate experience, could turn this powerful business model into something wholesome and effective that could work for me.

Which is exactly what I've done.

Before we get into the nitty gritty of the book and my systematic approach, or even any further into this introduction, I want to let you know that I did not give up my job, I did not invest my life savings and I didn't take any risks whatsoever in order to make this work for me. All I did was swap some free time to do a little extra work, and over time I turned that into a life-changing income.

That was 20 years ago. Now, I want to share my experience and help as many people as possible break out of the corporate structure and take ownership of their income and financial future.

I have spent a lot of time turning all the things I have learned over the years into systems and processes that mirror the way the corporate world works, so that people like you, who are used to operating in that way, can make the transfer.

For those of you who don't want to go all the way and abandon all the hard work you have done working your way up, then this system can provide a valuable second income that supplements that steady salary. The systems and processes allow you to plan your path according to the time you can allocate to building whatever level of business suits you.

Before we finish, I do want to cover the current climate of uncertainty in the aftermath of COVID-19 and its global effect. It has really shone a light on the frailty of the world and proved that nothing is truly safe.

Sadly, this applies to the entire corporate system, which has been turned upside down by these events. So many people are going to be facing hard times as the world's economies restart.

Of course, the corporation still has its place, but for those bright, hardworking individuals out there, there should be more reward for their hard work—they shouldn't have to fear that they will be suddenly left high and dry, as so many have been.

It's my intention to present you with the perfect solution. A business that you can develop part time that will give you the opportunity to earn a parallel income and can, at some point, become something you can turn into a stunning wealth creation tool.

Now don't be fooled! There's hard work involved and quite rightly so. The difference in this scenario is that you will be able to easily quantify just how effective that hard work is. What's more, as you maintain that hard work, you will begin to activate the exponential earning potential that my system can provide.

So, if like me, you are a corporate person, succeeding in that framework but looking around at the world and wondering how you can protect yourself against unforeseen events that could pull the rug out from underneath you, then this book is for you.

If you are worried that 45 years in work still won't cover the cost of the retirement you would like, then this book is for you.

If you're motivated and proactive, consistent and persistent, but the corporate ladder is just not letting you jump enough rungs at a time, then this book is for you.

If you can visualise a future where you eventually have to work less to earn more, but you're prepared to graft to get there, then this book is for you.

I want to get you out of the mindset that it's 'corporate life or bust' and into the mindset of parallel income and then into the mindset of financial freedom and all the benefits that come with it!

If this book resonates with you, and you'd like to explore the possibilities of having your own home-based business to experience entrepreneurial freedom for yourself, then visit www.CliffWalker.com/Consultation to schedule a Complimentary Home-Based Business Assessment Consultation (Value £375.00).

To your success,

Cliff Walker
The World's #1 Authority On Building A Global Home Business

CHAPTER 1

"The Only Way To Achieve Financial Freedom And Security Is Through The Safety And Security Of A Corporate Career"

The term financial freedom gets bandied about quite a lot these days as some sort of definitive cash amount that allows people to do whatever they like or live however they like. But when you really think about it, what is financial freedom? How do you define it?

A lot of it comes down to lifestyle and lifestyle choices that you want to make or are forced to make. In general, as your lifestyle grows, your need for relative income (in order to afford that life) grows, too.

At a certain income level and age, a £2,000 car might be aspirational. Ten years down the line, a £40,000 car might be aspirational. In both instances you need to be earning enough to afford to purchase them or repay a loan on those amounts.

If true financial freedom exists, it's the ability to pay for these cars without giving them a second thought. Let's face it, even if you won the lottery, that is a finite amount and each purchase you make dwindles your supply. Therefore, while it offers some momentary financial freedom, you're never technically free.

Given this simple logic, it's important we understand financial freedom, as it exists for those people who need to generate income. For people like you and me, financial freedom is the knowledge that our income is consistent and consistently increasing in order to provide the lifestyle we deem necessary to really enjoy our lives and create better lives for our loved ones.

For the majority of people, however, true financial freedom isn't a goal they actually set their minds on. Instead, they consider it simply the accumulation of time spent in work, which they trade for a pension they have to live within, for the rest of their days.

If that's your definition of financial freedom and you've made peace with it, then great! It's the same for the vast majority of the population.

I personally want a good deal more than that. If you do too, then read on.

I Can't Start A Business, I Need The Security Of A Corporate Job

This is such a common theme in the world today and no doubt the reason that the majority of people on this planet work for other people (more on this later).

I understand how you feel about needing a corporate job. I worked for more than 20 years, plugging away at the corporate dream, and loved every minute of it. I worked for great companies with great benefits, travelled the world and climbed up dozens of those infamous corporate rungs.

Working as I did, in Hammersmith, London, at the time, I used to be in the office at 7:30 am to avoid the traffic and leave again about 7:00 pm. Home in bed by 9:30 pm, ready for the 5:00 am alarm to do it all over again. Every single day of the week.

Of course, we do it for the benefits. Paid holidays, guaranteed money, a nice company car, sick pay and working towards the inevitable retirement when we can finally kick back and relax.

Change Your Mindset, Change Your Life

You can't scroll for more than two seconds on any social media site without seeing a post from someone about being positive or developing mind-power or manifestation. All which I'm a big fan of.

But I'm also a practical person who knows that everyone has bills to pay, and no amount of positive affirmations will magically make the water board lower my rates.

What I am really keen on is opportunity and giving yourself the opportunity to change your situation by taking action. But before we do that, it's important to have some understanding. The understanding allows us to see the bigger picture when it comes to income generation.

For the vast majority of the planet, income generation is linear. A straight line that involves regular payments from your employer that occasionally increase (or decrease) depending on your situation. This is really a trade situation because you are trading your time for that money.

The second type of income is leveraged income. This is where you are able to generate income from a number of different places at once.

The classic example is McDonalds. They have replicated their business model and have locations across the globe, all doing pretty much the same things and all generating income.

This type of income is vastly faster at generating bigger sums and it's not dependent on one person. If the owner of McDonalds worldwide gets ill, all the outlets don't stop trading. If one restaurant in the UK shuts down, the rest are still operating.

The third type of income is residual income. This is where you do some work and continue to earn from it over time.

There are some simple examples of this. One of the most common examples, and perhaps the easiest to understand, is music-related. If you write a hit song, you can earn money each time it is played on the radio. You only did the work a single time, but the income the song generates is residual.

Linear income is where it's at for most of the population. It's safe, simple and reliable. At least it used to be.

Sadly, the coronavirus outbreak has not only been a threat to life in a very real way but also our attempts to contain it have had a significant impact on the economies of the world. So much so that the safety we once sought in our linear income-based, corporate stronghold suddenly doesn't seem so safe.

Perhaps it's time to expand your knowledge on wealth creation, so you can take decisive action to protect yourself and your loved ones in the long term.

Cashflow Quadrant

I could try and give you my own version of income generation, but there's really no point when businessman and best-selling author Robert Kiyosaki has already created an elegantly simple way of illustrating how wealth is created.

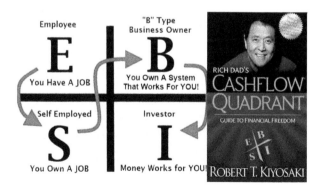

The cashflow quadrant is a very easy to understand schematic that plots the world of wealth generation in just four steps. As you can see, we can plot our income sources using this system too.

Starting from the top left, we have our linear income, the employees or self-employed of the world. The left side of the cashflow quadrant houses 95% of the population. Incredibly, despite housing so many people, this particular quadrant generates only 5% of the world's wealth.

Think about that for a second.

Based on those two very clear-cut and easy to understand figures, can you genuinely see yourself creating financial freedom as an employee?

This is the realisation I had, even when I was at the top of my game 20 years ago on a salary of nearly 200k. Even at that stage, I knew there was more out there. A different way to live, a different way to earn.

Anyway, getting back to the diagram, those inside the employee quadrant are generating wealth for business owners. Below employees, you have the self-employed, who own their own jobs but give up some of the perks of employment contracts for the potential to create a few of their own rules and the potential to earn in a less linear way.

However, whether you are an employee or self-employed, the reality is that YOU are the focal point of income generation, and that's not the safest place to be!

On the top right we have a change of tack, the business owners of this world. They utilise the two left-sided quadrants to create wealth for the businesses they own. Business owners typically understand how to leverage a business model to create income from many places.

Below that, on the bottom right, are the investors. These people use their wealth to generate more wealth, leveraging money to make more money.

So whereas on the right you have people trading time for money, on the right you have the power of leverage. And 95% of wealth is created here!

Like I said, this is a very simple example, and I want to use it to highlight how money is made and how you, as a human being of unlimited potential, armed with this information, could make some choices that enable you to move across this quadrant and live a life that is a little less ordinary.

It stands to reason that, in order to be financially free, you have to be somewhere on the right of the cashflow quadrant, creating some of the 95% of the wealth that exists there.

Remaining on that left side leaves you limited.

Just remember, I'm not asking you to leap over to the right and risk everything. I am saying you can steadily make your way there while keeping all of the benefits you enjoy in the top left corner. It's the best of both worlds.

The Income Mindset

I'm going to throw some more mindset shifting ideas at you to try and get this to sink in. The quadrants in the diagram describe a physical system that exists, and it's very easy for me to say, "Oh yeah, just look at this and make your mind up."

I appreciate that it's nowhere near as simple as that in real life.

When I was a very, very young man, I left school and got a job. My father, who had worked hard his entire life, drilled it into me that the way to get ahead in life was to work hard and make your way. Pay your dues and earn the right to move up.

It was sound advice, and even today I think of it because hard work is most definitely the answer. Unfortunately, my father didn't realise there was another way or that the majority of the cash that was up for grabs in the world just couldn't be reached from that side of the fence.

I'm absolutely certain that, if I had the conversation with him that I am having with you now—and it wouldn't be so one-sided, that's for sure—he would tell me that with a family to provide for, the risks in moving over to the right hand side of the quadrant would be too great.

And of course, he would be right. I had a great upbringing and I thank him wholeheartedly.

The difference, as I see it, is simply mindset-related and then down to a few practical steps. You don't need a job, you need income.

It's the income that pays the bills, the credit card, and the mortgage. You can easily replace one form of income with another, as long as you don't try and leap from one to the other.

With this in mind, what would be the most sensible way to make a transition? It would be to run two income streams concurrently until one can replace the other, right?

Totally a no-brainer.

What if I told you I can give you all the tools you need to do this, with no risk and only a minimal investment? There's some work involved, of course, but it wouldn't be any fun if there weren't!

You need to be prepared to devote 8-10 hours per week to a new business, and you can create something that will change your life forever.

Key Takeaways

- Reflect on the cashflow quadrant and where you are on it. Where would you like to be?

- Have a think about income. Understand that you can achieve it in multiple ways.

- Consider the values that the cashflow quadrant presents: 95% of people working away, generating just 5% of the wealth in the world.

- You have the power to take control of this situation and build something serious and sustainable with your free time.

CHAPTER 2

"The Corporate Promotion Track Is The Only Way To Build A Thriving Career"

Recent events have blown a bit of a hole in the stability of the corporate ladder and the opportunities it is able to offer the world. Some companies have fallen by the wayside through no fault of their own, while others are thriving.

The upshot is that there are absolutely no guarantees and, if anything, getting to the upper echelons of the corporate structure is just a little harder now, with companies streamlining and high-level positions becoming fewer and further between.

Consequently, there isn't the safety in climbing that ladder that could have been perceived just a matter of months ago. Whether or not you believe in the safety of it is actually bye-the-bye at this point.

The issue is, and always has been, that creating a business from scratch requires superhuman levels of effort, significant investment and ditching everything you have worked for up until now. It also means that no matter your skill level, no matter how good the product, there is always an element of risk, a risk that could cost you your life savings and potentially put you way back on your corporate career track.

45-Year Plan

We've spoken a lot about mindset, and that really is the biggest element of all when it comes to your financial future. What a lot of people aren't able to do is zoom out of the day-to-day and consider their lives as a big picture.

If you can do this and section off the significant elements workwise, you'll see that the biggest chunk of your life, for most people, is spent grafting away at one job.

If you are lucky, the location of that job may change and the logo on top of the pay slip may change. If you're really lucky, the job may get a bit easier as you get nearer to the 45-year mark.

Then, after all of those years, you get some time off. If you're lucky, you can afford to live on whatever you've got left in the bank and a reduced portion of the salary you've been on for those years.

When I worked for Diageo (then United Distillers), our office used to be in Hammersmith. For any of you who don't know Hammersmith, it's a bustling, busy district of London.

I was a typical commuter, living 50 miles or so away. I'd leave the house in the early hours to avoid the rush hour and then leave late in the evening.

Less than two hours after getting home, I'd be in bed, ready for another early morning. I used to look forward to the school holidays because there would be less traffic on the roads.

That's a bit sad, isn't it?

When I looked at my life in this way, even as a very well-paid corporate executive, I thought it looked a little like a prison sentence. Where, with good behavior, I might get out and live a little before I died.

Under normal circumstances I would apologise for painting such a bleak picture, but I'm here to reinforce that picture because it's absolutely the truth.

Now, to offer you a solution…

Parallel Income

The most important takeaway that you need to take from the start of this book is that you fully understand we want to give you the tools to start your business with us as a parallel income. The idea being that you are protected against risk and are helped by building income consistently.

You can see how the system works, how it grows, how you can enjoy a second income, and then how to carefully replace one income stream that is linear and relatively unchanging with another that you are truly excited about, which continues to grow and grow.

It's all in the planning. As I mentioned in my introduction, I have created a system which gives my business model significant structural detail and frameworks so that it can be utilised in any number of degrees, from those with minimal time all the way up to those people prepared to take it full-time.

This framework allows you, as a business owner, to plan in great detail exactly how you will execute each stage in order to build the income you want to enhance your life—all while striking the ultimate work-life balance. Inside the framework there is inherent flexibility, as I know only too well that real life ebbs and flows with busy periods, less busy periods and utterly manic, no-time-at-all periods.

With the framework in mind, I then encourage those I mentor to think of a three- to five-year plan. It involves a very realistic look at their work-life balance and then some projections about what we can achieve within that time frame.

Then, that plan is further broken down into quarterly goals, monthly goals and weekly work plans. This is no different than the planning that goes on for the business you currently work for.

Any big corporation will have a three- to five-year plan, and each department will have projections and plans to execute. Finally, you as an employee get your KPIs, which you work towards ahead of each appraisal.

The big difference in this instance is that this will be YOUR business, where YOU earn the money and YOU are in charge of how everything runs. There will be more on the business itself as we progress. I just want you to understand how all of this is related to mindset.

Once you have addressed how you feel about a parallel income and making small changes now, which will affect your life in big ways later on, then you are well on your way to a much brighter future.

Key Takeaways

- The corporate ladder is a great way to make a living, but it's not a great way to live the fullness of life.

- Trading 45 years of hard work for a reduction in salary for the rest of your days doesn't seem like a fair trade to me. Does it to you?

- In three to five years, you can transform your life through a significant adjustment to your finances. Now is the time to start.

- I can provide you with not just the tools, but the framework, planning and personal KPIs to succeed and thrive, starting with a parallel income.

CHAPTER 3

"It Is Impossible To Make Money In The First Two Years Of Building A Home-Based Business"

D epending on the literature you read, making money from a home business can take anywhere from two to five years.

For most people making the transition, there is the added complexity of learning a new skill, gaining a new certification, or buying products and building a client base. This generally incurs marketing costs, which can be compounded by the need to satisfy debtors as time elapses before profits are made.

It's a really tough gig.

Now imagine that you had a product ready to be shipped, marketing materials at your disposal, the backup of a billion-dollar company and mentorship from an individual who has not only thrived in the business but also helped construct the very fabric it has been built from.

Sounds a bit more promising, doesn't it?

Expanding Circles

I usually ask people the question, "If you won the lottery, what would you do with the money?"

And everybody pretty much knows exactly what they would do with the money if they were fortunate enough to win the lottery. And the first thing almost everyone says is, "I will quit my job."

How sad is that? We are spending all of our time in a place that we will ditch as soon as we have enough money. That thought alone should be enough to make you reevaluate your work-life balance.

Once I've highlighted this strange disparity that most people have, I go on to drill down and get an idea of what else exists within that paradigm of what people want versus what they can potentially have.

The way I do this is to explain that everyone has two circles in their lives. One circle is big and contains all the things you would like to own, accomplish and experience— this is your dream circle. Then, you've got a smaller circle.

Can you guess what that is? Well, that's your income circle. For the vast majority of the population, their income circle is smaller than their dreams circle.

Sadly, what happens is that people shrink their dreams circle to fit their income circle rather than expanding their income circle so they can achieve their dreams. I then say to people that my business can provide them with the circle-expanding jolt they need in order to live a much fuller life.

Pay Rise Mindset

When developing your parallel income, it's important to stage your progress and not get carried away with the potential on offer.

Yes, there are huge rewards, but you must put the work in to get there. It's a real business which requires effort to build. I like to keep people grounded by reminding them of the path they are currently on and the time it has taken to get to the stage they are in.

Let's say you're making, £45,000 a year in your current career, and let's also say that you have been working in that career for 20 years. So, it's taken you 20 years to get to £45,000 in annual income.

It's unrealistic to begin earning £45,000 per month immediately. What we *can* do is look into creating a 12-month plan which could, if all goes well, match that annual salary of £45,000.

More realistically, as a parallel income, we would be aiming for £22,500. Now, I don't know about you, but I think the chances of your boss offering you a 50% pay rise are pretty minimal. However, this is achievable with the right tools, mindset and actions.

THE ENTREPRENEUR MINDSET SHIFT

Income + Leveraged Income = Financial Freedom

We've already spoken about creating wealth and which side of the cash quadrant you would like to be on. Part of building your own business involves taking responsibility for your own income.

For those people starting regular businesses like shops, cafés, PR companies, garages—you get the picture—they all have to do all kinds of projections in order to forecast a profit, and then they have to manage all kinds of variables in order to succeed in achieving it.

The business I am proposing that you start offers a much faster track to success. There is, of course, a product to sell, but it is a fully-formed product with marketing material and the backing of a billion-dollar company (more on this later), but it also has one more key component—leveraged income.

We touched on this briefly in Chapter 1, using the classic example of franchises and McDonald's. This business model allows the owners of McDonald's to generate income from every one of their restaurants without having to physically run every one of them.

Individuals purchase those mini-businesses and generate their own income, whilst paying McDonald's for the right to sell their burgers.

There are some other elements which make the franchise a fantastic model as well, in as much as the brand name is instantly recognisable and the marketing is centralized, so the franchisee needn't worry about that part of the business.

The business that I want you to create has many of the same features and allows you to create leveraged income by creating a team of business owners who will generate income for you. In this way, with the split between selling the product and creating a team and having fellow business owners, you can begin to create your very own leveraged income.

This enables you to scale your income in a way that simply cannot be matched by traditional business models.

The Automobile Analogy

The way I like to explain this business to people is that it's very much like pushing a car. The first push is the hardest. Getting it rolling takes considerable effort. However, once the car is rolling, you can keep it going with relative ease.

This business works in a very similar way. You need to expend the most effort getting into a suitable enough state that you can then begin to hang back a little and just push the business to keep it moving forward. You obviously do need to keep it rolling because, should it slow down, much like the car, you will need to use that much larger effort to get it back up to speed.

Key Takeaways

- Consider your two circles: are your income and dreams in sync?

- Would a 50% pay rise make a difference to your life? Consider what you would do with that extra cash.

- Building a business is like pushing a car—you need to put in some serious effort at the start, but the payoff is worth it.

- Taking advantage of leveraged income allows you to have the best of both worlds—a business with customers and leveraged income.

CHAPTER 4

"In Order To Build A Successful Business, You Must Quit Your Job To Make It All Happen"

The issue I have with this myth is that it's been built up over so long that it's almost become some sort of entrepreneurial mantra. The idea that you have to throw away your old life and create a new one where you dedicate your life to the business.

Of course, the myth has been built because so many people have done it this way. When you break it down, for lots of people, there's some truth in the sheer scale of work that business owners have to achieve.

If you want to really run a business, doing all the things that a traditional business owner needs to do, then yes, you probably need about 60 hours a week to get a business from zero to profit. You may also need about five years and a ton of cash.

Part of the myth is built on a predication that pressure is part of the process, that pressure accompanies all types of entrepreneurial endeavor.

There's pressure to succeed or rather to be seen as successful. The cars, the house, the suits, the holidays. Then there's the almost overwhelming pressure of putting it all on the line.

Coming up with the cash for a new venture is pressure. Spending it all on a business is pressure. Trying to turn a profit is pressure.

Surviving the pressure is part of the game. But it doesn't have to be that way. …

All The Assets

What if, instead of all that pressure, the product range was already developed?

The entire R&D has been done, the packaging, the testing, the manufacture, and the infrastructure. What if the marketing materials were in place, with incredible fact sheets, videos and expert endorsements? What if you even had the shipping sorted so that your customers can get the product you sell them in no time at all from a central location, but you still get the profit?

It sounds a bit like a franchise, doesn't it? Well, what if the business you start had all the benefits of a franchise without any of the huge costs (typically they are £50k+)? What if the company offering this opportunity was on course to become as big as Apple and Amazon and had already surpassed a billion dollars in annual sales using the business model I am proposing?

It's an exciting proposition, isn't it? It takes all of the pressure away and replaces it with excitement. Instead of having thousands of items on your to-do list and feeling like you're treading water and close to losing it all, you have a feeling of incredible positivity.

What's more, with the continual progress that you can achieve with the assets we give you, there is the opportunity to seriously outpace the growth of even the most ambitious startups.

Mentorship

I am very proud to say that I have spent 20 years using this business model. I have seen everything on my way up through the ranks, and what is even more pertinent to you as a new business owner is that I started the same way that you are. I was a corporate guy, and I took to this system and really made it work for myself.

One of the many benefits of being part of this business is that you will have me as a mentor. I will be there to help guide you through everything—and trust me when I say I have been there and seen it all. I am now, thanks to this business model, a seven-figure annual earner, and I want to help you get there too.

It's absolutely not a quick fix, but the leveraged income means that once you gain momentum, the rewards come thick and fast.

For those joining us on this journey, there are all kinds of benefits in the form of training, webinars, books, and, of course, the mentor system.

Leave The Technical Stuff To The Experts

The beauty of being in this industry and having the benefit of a big company backing you is that you don't need to be a product expert. You don't need to be able to field every question from every potential customer. We have experts that can do that for you, and there are YouTube videos and detailed fact sheets.

This drastically shortens the learning curve and instills even more confidence in our business owners. What's more, it lends even more credibility to you as an independent business owner and a team builder.

Breaking It Down

We've already spoken about parallel income. We've already discussed the combination of selling products directly and finding other like-minded entrepreneurs for leveraged income. We've also talked about having a mentor.

Right now, for someone approaching the business, it might still feel a little lacking in detail. Now, I'm not going to explain everything here and now; however, I want you to know that this isn't a system that's been developed which allows for failure. It has been specifically designed to promote success.

With that in mind, like any great business, there has to be some considerable planning involved. Luckily, having done this for so long, I can save you heaps of time.

I can help you create a 12-month, parallel income plan which we can then break down into monthly, weekly and daily actions. Which, if you stick to, will enable you to create a new financial world for yourself.

For those of you who have read Steven Covey's book, *The Seven Habits of Highly Effective People* (which I heartily recommend), you'll be pleased to know we start with the end in mind. We will look at where you want to be in 12 months and use that as an action plan to work backwards and create our action. Then, each step of the way we can tick off our achievements and reach our goals.

Alongside these goals, I also like to do some timetabling because, in order to accomplish these tasks, you need to make time. For those starting out in the business, this can be the toughest factor.

You have to commit to the actions and then timetable when you will complete the actions that lead to the goals.

Doing it alongside your corporate job (at least to start with) is what will make a bit tougher. But the payoff will be worth it.

Going back to our car analogy from the last chapter, the work you put in at the beginning is getting the machine moving. You can't give it a push one Monday and then again two weeks later and expect to get it rolling. You have to dedicate time to get the momentum up and then the work becomes easier.

Key Takeaways

- Think about pressure and what kind of business you would like to own.

- Consider the model I am proposing. The entire business is in place before you begin—the only missing piece is you.

- Splitting your time between acquiring customers and team building gives you the opportunity to earn linear, leveraged AND residual income.

- Having a mentor can help you be productive and profitable, right from the get-go.

CHAPTER 5

"Quitting A Job To Pursue Building A Business Is Risky, And It Will Be Perceived That You Are Taking A Step Back In Your Career"

I come across this attitude quite a lot, and I have absolute empathy.

For most people, the desire to create a business is counterbalanced by the desire to stay solvent, and there are very few times one can leap from full-time corporate work to an entrepreneurial initiative.

What's more, people's attitudes are generally quite negative, so any time that you make noises about wanting to start up on your own; you only hear how hard it would be.

It's tough to clear your headspace enough to know deep-down whether a business idea will really work. Let alone whether you can weather the financial storm.

It stands to reason that the very best way to make the leap, were it possible, would be to develop the business while you're still working. Thus, you would eliminate much of the risk.

How Many Redundancies?

Years ago, I worked with a lovely lady named Jane, who was one of the most proactive employees I'd ever seen. She was diligent, motivated, forward-thinking, and energetic.

She was a model employee in every respect. We worked together for some years, and she left to go to another firm.

Many years later, we bumped into one another, and I was expecting to reconnect with my live-wire colleague. Instead I caught up with a different woman.

Unbelievably, she had been on a run of poor fortune workwise and had been made redundant four times within five years.

She was absolutely gutted. Unfortunately, she'd just keep going to companies that promised a lot and then didn't deliver—they weren't even able to stay afloat to keep her going.

Obviously, she then enquired about me, and I was able to tell her about the way that I was now working. She was amazed at the business model and staggered at the progress I had made.

Needless to say, I mentored her for a short while, and she went off and earned enough to make her retirement a lot more fun—without any of the worries that come with corporate uncertainty.

The point I'm trying to illustrate here is that working for big companies in no way guarantees your financial safety or mental well-being. Jane had gone from absolute superstar to extremely upset in five short years. All her ideas about job security had been severely knocked, and that anxiety had crept into her home life.

When you're unsure if you'll have a job next year, you don't particularly feel like planning a holiday or buying a new car. It's no way to live.

The Ultimate Side Hustle

With world economies shrinking on a vast scale as the fallout from COVID-19 continues, now has never been a better time to protect yourself with a comprehensive side hustle.

For those of you who have no idea what I'm talking about, a side hustle is youthful vernacular for a side project or second income. A Plan B.

Entrepreneurial proponents of this idea are wide-ranging, and ideas for good side hustles have virtually become a viral internet theme. The idea being that individuals, couples and families become aware of and take action to ensure their own financial security.

The side hustle is a private business that you build stealthily and then reveal when you've achieved your dreams. Whether that dream is a new car, new house, retirement—whatever.

The point is that you take charge and use your time in such a way as to maximise the financial yield from your time.

In particular, the partners and family element of this viral phenomenon are exceptionally motivating. Here, couples and parents are combining their efforts to create something together. It is simultaneously a hustle and a bonding experience. It helps cement the relationship, introduce life-skills and creates the idea of legacy.

I'm a huge fan of the side hustle, and part of my reason for writing this book was to contribute to the potential that this movement has for instigating change and creating financial freedom for hard-working people.

The New Normal

I don't know about you, but I'm getting kind of tired of this phrase, but it's utterly on point. We now have a new normal in the wake of COVID-19.

For a huge swathe of people, that means they are now working from home. The office is out of bounds. This brings with it all kinds of new discoveries. New tech, for example. Zoom has done pretty well out of this, haven't they?

You may have also discovered that getting the job done doesn't necessarily require eight continuous hours of laptop time. And now the commute is gone, there's some extra time there, too. What if you could use those extra minutes to earn as much as you do from your day job?

It's an exciting prospect, and one worth considering.

Key Takeaways

- Quitting your job is not the answer.

- Having a job does not guarantee your financial safety.

- The side hustle is your protection against the whims of the world. Build something amazing.

- The new normal is here. How much time could you devote to changing your life?

CHAPTER 6

"In Order To Be Able To Cope And Succeed As An Entrepreneur, You Must Have A Degree In Business Or An MBA"

As you know, I love taking people from the corporate world and introducing them to this business model. It gives me great pleasure to help reinvent them in a new paradigm. But that's not to say that it doesn't come with same fear and doubts that occur in those corporate jobs.

Most commonly, I come up against the fear of rejection. There's a tendency for people starting their own businesses to assume that, in order to succeed, they must be the world's greatest salesperson, that they should, through some incredible trickery and mastery, be able to convince anyone and everyone to buy their product or service.

Out of interest, do you think Bill Gates is a master salesperson? What about Elon Musk or Steve Jobs?

No? So, what did they do?

They created great products, and more importantly than that, they believed in them. Such was their unwavering belief and commitment that they were able to change the world with their products.

The other misconception about business and selling is that you HAVE to be a Bill Gates or Elon Musk. You don't. They are one-offs.

To be successful you have to be YOU. The best version of you. Authentic. Proactive. Positive. That's it.

Let me give you a scenario. You are out to lunch. It's a lovely day, and you've sat outside and had a beautiful salad which you've paired with a lovely glass of white wine. The waiter approaches the table and offers you another glass of that beautiful, cool, crisp, French wine. You say, 'no thanks,' knowing that, despite the perfect conditions for a top-up, you are driving.

Now, does the waiter leave that scene with his head in his hands cursing his salesmanship? Absolutely not. Both you and he know that the offer was a professional courtesy—you had a need that he could potentially fill, and he offered to do it.

Unfortunately, the timing wasn't right. On another day you would have said yes. Today, however, you politely declined.

This is a fact of the world. Why should selling a product or introducing a business be any different? Why would your mind set you up to be dismayed every single time someone declines your offer?

Sounds like madness, doesn't it? And yet, that's how many people's minds work.

In business, when you have a product, it's your duty to present it in the best light possible and overcome objections if you need to. What you can't do is force people to say yes. More to the point, no one is expecting you to.

The New ABC: Always Be Captivating

The old catchphrase for a salesperson was Always Be Closing, the ABCs of the shark in a suit, smelling out deals and pouncing on the weaker-minded. It's a very old way of thinking, and yet the perception persists.

For those without the supposedly prerequisite jaw full of razor-sharp teeth, fear of feeling foolish is a problem. It is another common thread I experience when I speak to people about creating their own business. People worry about how they will be perceived, and this speaks to an insecurity that we all have deep down.

The way to approach this is to have confidence in the product and simply be the best version of yourself so that you come across with authentic enthusiasm. Luckily, in this line of work, the products are backed by a wildly successful company, so all of the insecurities that could potentially affect the budding entrepreneur can simply melt away.

Going back to our successful business leaders, they all oozed confidence and their products were the real star of the show. It's no different here. By trusting in the product and the business model, you can concentrate on being yourself and casting aside the doubts that other business owners have to deal with.

This business, like almost every other, is built upon relationships. In this day and age, these take all manner of forms, mostly electronic. You already nurture these in any number of forms online.

When it comes to building a business, it's simply a variant of those existing networks, connections and relationships. You build them the same way you do in real life, by being authentic and genuine.

Finally, the support that is given is second to none. There are systems, processes, training and development that are all geared to help you succeed. Running your own business isn't about finding ways to trip you up; it's about finding ways to help you flourish, and I can certainly help you there.

Fail To Prepare, Prepare To Fail

This is a mantra that has taken shape in almost every walk of life. Whether you are studying, playing sports, buying a home or building a business, there is always the fear of failure, but being prepared completely negates the option. When you are armed with the right tools, you can approach any task with courage and conviction.

It's the first step in my training programme, and I draw on all of my years of experience to show new business owners how to navigate those first few weeks. I know first-hand each and every question you will have, and I have an answer for it. More than that, I have tools that will help you understand the answer to the question and how then to answer it.

Going back to our automobile metaphor, I can literally give you the strength to do that first push so you can get the wheels in motion. You are then trundling along, ready to add some acceleration of your own.

Collaboration Is Key

Interconnectivity is a watchword for this century. We've seen the world shrink in front of our very eyes. I am writing this from my home office in South Africa, and you could be reading it from the UK, Australia or the US—even in the air as you travel between them.

You could be anywhere. I could be anywhere. The world is so small that it doesn't matter where we are.

Similarly, it doesn't matter where your customers or new team members are. This interconnectivity enables us to maintain and grow relationships independently of geographical location.

It also enables us to share information really effectively. I can have a face-to-face meeting with you, send you PDFs, share videos, and connect with you in innumerable ways.

So there's never a time when you are on your own toughing it out.

Similarly, when you begin to build your collaborative marketing business, you are never far away from your customers or team members. It means that the whole process is interconnected.

With that in mind, I offer a framework you can not only follow but also pass on to those you choose to join your team. Its collaborative strength is based on a system that I use every day. I'm not going to give you the full lowdown here, but I will give you a flavor of what it entails.

The framework consists of six master tasks that need to be completed in order to build a successful business. These master tasks are focused on the following key areas:

1) Strategy

2) Daily method of operation

3) Personal growth and training

4) Team development

5) Leadership

6) Culture

No doubt you've come across similar frameworks in your day job. They are there to provide you with all the details you need to be successful. Each of these master tasks has a set of subtasks, and then within those, there are actions that need to be taken.

Here you can see that this model, like any other business model, has a systematic theme and a core method that facilitates forward motion and the building blocks of a business you can use to change your life. What's incredibly useful is that outside of the framework, running alongside to enhance your capabilities, are seminars and talks from business owners across the globe sharing their stories.

Additionally, there are product packages which allow you to tap into the billion-dollar company that is providing you with your core products. It's a fantastic, interconnected global environment that will nurture your thirst for success in a way that no other business can rival.

Enrol, Don't Recruit

One final word on collaboration. There's a tendency for old-school mannerisms and ideas to proliferate the perception of this business model.

As we've talked about, the need to build a team stems from this idea of leveraged income. You build a team and earn from their success—in the same way that McDonald's builds new restaurants and other people run them. It allows you to focus on two elements, selling the product and teaching others to do the same.

In the old days, this was often misconstrued as some sort of recruitment drive that involved coercing and cajoling. Of course that's never been the case with our model. In our interconnected world we don't recruit anyone, we enrol them.

The difference is a key point and can be explained in a similar way to our analogy of the waiter asking you if you want more wine. He doesn't make you have another drink, and he certainly doesn't pour it for you and assumptively bring it to the table. He simply offers you the opportunity to have another drink, which depending on your circumstances, leads to a yes or no answer.

The same is true when it comes to enrolment. You present a connection with the information from this book, and people decide whether to enrol on your team.

It really is that simple.

Key Takeaways

- Interconnectivity has already provided you with any number of social circles and relationships. Starting a business is simply starting a new network.

- Always Be Captivating! When you believe in something, you don't need to sell.

- Frameworks already exist that can guide you from your very first day.

- Enrolment is a key part of the business, and your passion will be the deciding factor, nothing else.

CHAPTER 7

"In Order To Build A Successful Home-Based Business, You Must Be Willing To Take A Significant Hit To Your Financial Resources"

The financial components of starting a new business are perhaps the most stressful. Even if you have a great product or service, while you build a customer base, you have to ask yourself what you are prepared to lose in terms of income and what you are prepared to spend in terms of marketing.

Add to that the cost of inventory, IT, premises, insurance, rates—all those things make for a dizzying list of demands on your personal resources. They all take up valuable real estate in your mind and make for a potentially volatile situation.

Expectation is also a key variable. The expectation to make money quickly can scupper your new business goals. Perhaps that's why so many new businesses fail.

Without wanting to labour the point, financial pitfalls are often what stop a bigger percentage of the population from starting their own enterprises. It's quite easy to retreat to the safety of a corporate contract with benefits like sick pay and guaranteed holiday pay.

If you add children and their security into the mix, suddenly the risks become seemingly too real. No one would want to compromise the safety and security of their children.

The other major downfall of new businesses comes from a lack of effective marketing. The cashflow issues that accompany the litany of demands on a new business invariably cause marketing to take a back seat when it should be one of the core elements.

Subsequently, you have shops full of product and no customers or a brilliant website and no traffic. Sadly, another casualty of the entrepreneur is the social life and network connections which are sacrificed for the 'expected' work ethic.

Own It

Creating a business from home is a decision that, for most people, just involves too many variables, such as product, shipping, sales, marketing, staff, growth, planning and culture.

It's also, for the majority of entrepreneurs, quite a lonely endeavor. The lone ranger, out on their own, up against the world. Add this to the financial pressure and you can understand why so few people take the leap.

Given the right circumstances, this situation can be wildly different. There are instances where the decision to create your own home business can create a situation full of positives. You can still have financial security, you can be fully supported by a team of experts, you can still have colleagues, and you can commit as much time as you need to the cause.

In the case of the opportunity I am presenting, I can offer all of these benefits and even more.

Develop The Skill Of Being Active And Engaged

There are, of course, some requirements that you will need to fulfil from the entrepreneur playbook that are part and parcel of every business owners' repertoire of skills and beliefs. These are the beliefs and behaviours that every business owner will tell you helped them overcome all the adversity that plagued their progress until the good times came.

In the case of my business, you won't need these skills to overcome adversity and survive hard times; you will need them to create something astonishing. And when I say that, I really mean it.

The onus is on you. You have to be responsible for the drive and determination that fuels the business. Yes, there are a ton of incredible support structures, processes and frameworks in place to make the process easier and more effective—but ultimately, like everything in life, the real clincher is your attitude.

If you take the opportunity that we are presenting and then use it, alongside the grit and determination and patience that you would for any other new business, then you will succeed and surpass even your wildest expectations.

I have a dedicated planning methodology which accompanies all of the members of my team. It is really the expression of all my years of experience in this field. Knowing this business as well as I do, it almost acts as a step-by-step guide to success.

If you combine this with a sensible and achievable plan that I provide, which will guide you through the earning milestones we set together, then you have a recipe that can deliver all of the benefits of entrepreneurial endeavour with the financial benefits of a business that is established and earning well.

What takes this situation and makes it even more incredible is the fact that the business structure on offer means that you become a member of my team, first and foremost. Additionally, the opportunity exists for you to surpass my level of success under your own steam; there are no corporate structures in place that prevent that happening (more on this in Chapter 9).

What I want you to get from this is the burning desire to surpass my success and to create your own business, team and even training materials to become bigger and better than I am. As we say, you're in business for yourself, but you're never by yourself.

Key Takeaways

- Most new businesses incur huge costs just simply getting a product or service to market.

- Develop the skill of being active and engaged.

- There are no barriers to success.

- You will be in business for yourself, but you will never be by yourself.

CHAPTER 8

"Building A Home-Based Business Is Extremely Difficult Due To Distractions, Interruptions And Lack Of A Structured Work Environment"

When I talk to my team members about working from home, none of them can believe the obstacles they put in their own way when they began the process. It's ridiculously easy to get distracted when you are at home.

Even a 20-year veteran like me can choose to give the kitchen a quick tidy rather than sit down and complete a task.

Luckily, I know how this little trick of the mind works, so it very rarely happens. Distractions are part and parcel of life in general. When you are at your day job, I'm sure it's easy to spend a few too many minutes having a chat with Karen while the kettle boils, but when there's a deadline to work to, you know you've got to get behind that desk and do the work.

There's no difference at home, you just need to be disciplined.

The current global reaction to COVID-19 has meant that more and more people have had to transition to a working-from-home paradigm. This bodes extremely well for those people looking to create a home-based business.

Luckily, in this particular business, you don't actually need any really specialised office equipment. You need a laptop or PC, which most people already have, and you might need a phone.

What you can decide to create, if you want, is a working zone. This is a space that you use to do your work—it's separate from the rest of your home life.

It doesn't need to be an entire room, just an area where you can go and complete your tasks. The idea being that simply by entering that space, you become work-oriented and step into the zone.

By doing so, you are less likely to get distracted and more likely to complete work tasks and then get back to being awesome in the rest of your life.

If you think of your work in this way, as a collection of tasks, you only need to work until these tasks are completed. Nobody is expecting you to be chained to a swivel chair for a set amount of time—that's not the point of the business at all. Time is irrelevant—you need it to do the important stuff but every other bit of it belongs to you.

The more effective (and subsequently successful) you become, the more time you can claim back as your own. Eventually, I want you to be able to give up the full-time job and work the hours that suit you best, earning more money while you do it!

I like to think of this process as a kind of enhanced time management. It's a case of being as productive as possible, which in turn is only possible if you are as organised as possible.

Luckily for you, as I mentioned before, I have all kinds of processes and frameworks which can help break down all the tasks you need to complete—and in such a way as to virtually walk you through the process.

Thanks to modern technology, you're never more than a click away from additional information, supporting videos and in the case of this business opportunity, a ton of incredibly well-designed marketing assets.

The element I like to focus on when I discuss this with my teams is that it's designed for you to find the positives and enjoy them. Using enhanced time management, you can create the time to meet friends for coffee, go to that football game, stay over after the concert and grab breakfast. All the things you couldn't really do when you were tied to the office job because they would cost you part of your free-time allowance, aka holiday entitlement.

It's really about changing the quality of your life and reshaping your perception of income, time and enjoyment. This business is designed to enhance your life.

To begin with, I want to supplement your income and give you the option to upgrade that holiday package or buy a new car. In time, I want to upgrade that position and give you the same income you have now for a fraction of the hours you are currently working. Finally, I want you to have a burning desire to create the ultimate work-life balance where you graft at unprecedented levels for concise bursts that keep the business healthy and your free time full of pleasurable pursuits.

For those of you with unbridled ambition like me—who decide to take this business model and push it—there are a host of incredible incentives and perks. You could be flown out to exotic locations, win prizes and much more.

Key Takeaways

- You don't need specialist equipment or swathes of cash to invest to get started in this business.

- Working from home can be tough, but most of us have some experience of it now.

- Create a space that allows you to concentrate and complete the actions that will lead to success.

- I am here to help you every single step of the way.

CHAPTER 9

"All Home Businesses Are Pyramid Schemes That Don't Work"

It's a sad fact that there are some negative associations when people consider the home-based business model. Many years ago, there were some unscrupulous salespeople who preyed on others using a system that benefited them greatly and lumbered their victims with some devalued goods.

Fortunately, those days are well behind us as pyramid schemes are illegal.

Network or collaborative marketing works in a completely transparent way and is simply a disruptive force against traditional marketing channels.

The traditional marketing model involves a company promoting their product in a variety of ways to drive people to a shop, destination, website, or some kind of buying decision. The ones we're all familiar with are TV adverts, billboards, radio averts, web ads and now social media feeds, which are full of adverts, too.

This is a generally accepted way to conduct marketing, and for each of those companies, there is a fixed cost when it comes to buying those spaces. If you want to have a billboard on a main road in London, there's a fixed cost for the length of time you want that advert. If you buy Instagram advertising, you select a target market and then Instagram delivers a number of impressions for a fixed cost.

For big companies who spread their marketing across all these platforms, the costs are astronomical and greatly affect the price you pay as a consumer.

What my business model offers is a marketing model that is dependent on all of the business owners, and as a result, it saves huge amounts of money. These savings are passed on to those business owners resulting in the earning potential I have been talking about.

Disruption Is Big Business

So, what is all this talk of disruption? Well, it's a big deal these days.

Disruption is where you have a classic way of doing something, and then a new business model comes in and disrupts it. The classic example is Amazon. They've disrupted the way we shop.

Normally, our need for specific goods would involve a trip in a car to a place, where we would buy a thing. Amazon has disrupted this market by providing a place where almost every product on earth can be reached, ordered and delivered with a couple of clicks on a phone or laptop.

Online shopping isn't the only example. Just Eat is disrupting the restaurant business, Uber is doing it with taxis, Reed did it with recruitment, Airbnb does it with hotels, Rightmove did it with selling houses, and then Purple Bricks swooped in and disrupted the estate agents again!

The list goes on and on.

The point is that disruption is the next marker for success. Network marketing or collaborative marketing is the disruptive force in sales and marketing.

Ask yourself if internet ads are effective. … Do you even see that many TV adverts now that you watch streaming services? When did a billboard wow you enough to make you Google the product?

Then there are all those products that seem like the one you want, but when they arrive, they really aren't. You chose it because it came up on your Amazon search as the cheapest version and you thought 'why not?'

They're not built the same, they don't have the right features and you realise you've been duped by the web and some unscrupulous seller. It's happened to me, more than once. Sometimes a bargain isn't a bargain if you have to buy the product twice.

What about personal recommendations? They're pretty good, right? If someone you know genuinely raves about a product and you've seen the results, you'd be interested right?

That's all network marketing is. Only I feel the disruptive element has become such that a new name should be offered up: collaborative marketing.

It's financially more sensible to let the product sell itself, and that's how confident this company is. You wouldn't do that if you were sending out iPhone cases claiming to be leather but that are really just cereal boxes cut up and painted red....

Where Are The Real Pyramids? You're In One Right Now.

Have you ever thought about the corporate structure you are in right now? In general, there is a single person at the top and then the team expands below with each person having more and more people under them.

What's interesting is that the person at the top also earns the most and the money dwindles as you move down the structure. Now, if you were to draw that structure from a single point at the top expanding as it spreads below it would look like... yes, that's right, a pyramid.

What's more, the pyramid you are in while you work for a corporation has a bunch of fail-safes in the structure to prevent the lower guys from reaching the top of the pyramid. You can only move up when one of the other members of the structure leaves, and it means that the opportunities to advance get less and less as you scale the building.

Ultimately it means fewer and fewer people earning the big bucks at the top, and more people at the bottom are earning less.

Flip The Pyramid

What you will discover in your first weeks with me is that the collaborative model is so transparent that you and I, despite the 20-year disparity in our time in the industry, will have access to the same products at the same prices. You will have exactly the same advancement opportunities as every other business owner, no matter how long they have been in the industry.

What this means is that, if you work hard, you will be rewarded in a totally transparent way. You won't have to wait for a promotion, you won't have to change your skillset to adapt to a role in order to move upward, and you will never have to wait your turn or pay your dues.

We've touched on this before, but it's worth reiterating—you also have access to all of the info, marketing materials, videos and samples as everyone else. It's a totally level playing field.

If the only deciding factor is your own determination, don't you think that this would be the perfect business model for you?

Key Takeaways

- Pyramid selling is illegal; it's an old-school term for something that doesn't even exist anymore.

- Strangely enough, you're probably in a pyramid right now. What are the chances you'll ever reach the top?

- Transparency is the key to this model; there is never a time when you won't know what you're earning or how it's done.

- There are literally no limits when it comes to this business model; if 100,000 are successful then the business is even more successful. There's no funnel, no filters and no stopping ambitious business owners.

CHAPTER 10

"Home Businesses Mean Begging Close Friends To Buy Products They Don't Want"

The collaborative business model isn't particularly well-understood by the general population; however, as soon as you mention that you want to start a business from home, everyone is an expert and can predict its immediate doom.

So let's start this chapter off by understanding some of the complexities of the traditional business model and comparing it to the home-based model.

Let's say you have a laboratory, kitchen, workshop or office and you dream up a product. It's a sure-fire winner, and you know it. So, you begin designing it.

Then you have to come up with suitable materials to make the product. You need to build a prototype so you can test that it works. Then you need to patent it to ensure the idea is legally yours.

The next step is to seek to manufacture the product. You have to think about pricing and the cost of manufacture, distribution, marketing, etc., so that you can project the kind of profit each and every unit could potentially generate for you.

You then have to get prices for the manufacture and make sure that the factory producing whatever you've dreamed up can either build them on demand or store up certain amounts so that you can expedite them to the various outlet channels you have in mind.

All the while this is going on, you have to decide how you want to sell your product. Are you going to create a web shop? Sell to a supermarket? Have you thought about packaging? Branding? Design?

Oh, hang on, we haven't touched on safety; your product must be safe to use or consume.

Right, now back to it…

You have your distribution sorted, but you need to negotiate the numbers so that the product is moved in scalable batches and you don't have extra warehousing costs as the product is made and then sold.

Finally, with all that work done, your product might end up in a shop or sold through a distributor. But maybe they're not really promoting your product, so you have to do some marketing on your own. You realise that's hugely expensive, and because you've used a third-party seller, your profit per unit doesn't really account for the additional marketing costs you are incurring.

As you can see, trying to juggle the entirety of this process as an entrepreneur requires significant knowledge and skill, not to mention the help and assistance of a swathe of experts and employees along the way if you plan to do it right.

When you think that there are so many companies vying for traction on Amazon, eBay or Etsy, you can see that there are myriad issues which can affect your success.

Home Is Where The Heart Is

The home business model alleviates 95% of these issues. You already have products, distribution channels, marketing materials, shipping, testing, safety and much more. What you as the business owner are responsible for is creating a small customer base and developing your own team of additional business owners and team-builders.

Each of them then goes on to do the same, but you get paid for each person they then introduce and the products they sell. So, in time, you can earn as others do from the endeavour of the team as a whole. It's a fantastic system and everyone is an equally valuable cog within it.

As you can see, our business model is just a little different. It's disruptive, as we discussed in Chapter 9, and that's because the old business models are falling by the wayside.

The world is changing. Working from home is the key to the new world and so are small but mighty networks of engagement. When you multiply those networks exponentially, you have a system that benefits more people and redistributes traditional marketing money directly to you, the marketeer.

It's a stunningly simple but effective solution to the modern retail challenge. Think of this system as the Amazon, Tesla, Airbnb or Uber of sales and marketing. What it can do for you is literally life changing.

We Don't Sell, We Inform

In this day and age, the idea of being a cold-blooded super-seller is just as outdated as having a physical keypad on a mobile phone. It's just not the done thing.

We all have so many connections and so much going on that it wouldn't be worth the effort of hounding someone to make a sale anyway.

What we do in this business is simply inform people of what we are up to.

To use a more old-school example: If you loved shoes and were really passionate about them, to the point where you opened your own shoe shop, you would tell your mates, right? You would hope that the next time they wanted shoes, they would do you a solid and stop to buy some new shoes. You wouldn't doorstep them, measure their feet and insist they bought some shoes, would you?

Of course not! And, if the shoes in your shop were competitively priced, you'd hope a few of your friends and family would buy some. What's more, if they did get a good deal from your shoe shop, you would hope that they would tell their friends and family to stop by.

This home business is absolutely no different. In fact, we are so confident in the product that we have free samples you can hand out when you need to.

It means that you can operate in exactly the same way as the shoe example: be passionate and tell your friends, family and connections what you are up to. When the time is right for them and their buying decisions, they will come to you.

The same applies for adding to your team. Inform, educate and share your enthusiasm and others will join you, as others are joining me. Person-to-person is more personal!

The other interesting and compelling element that this business model brings up is that, since we are selling in a more direct way of person-to-person, there has to be more trust in the products.

I already touched on the race to the bottom that exists when it comes to internet products and the endless price pinching that leads to poor purchasing decisions and sub-par products. The issue here is that, despite the seemingly useful rating system, we are all guilty of trying to get the best price and sometimes that leads to poor decision making—and there are plenty of companies whose entire business model is snaring those of us making snap decisions.

When it comes to trusting quality, what better recommendation is there than the genuine feedback you get from a satisfied customer who tells a friend how happy they are with a product? In this day and age, it's actually priceless.

When you become a business owner, you want the product you are promoting to be so good that you can let it speak for itself. You want people's reaction to be such that, without knowing it, they are effectively selling it for you.

Do you think a business like this could exist selling products that everyone complains about? Would you invest your own time and energy into such products?

Of course not! Would I bother to write an entire book if I knew that, at some point down the line, I would get found out and face the potential backlash of thousands of disgruntled people? No way.

So please take heart from these words and the existence of a billion-dollar company which believes in its products so much that it is prepared to have thousands of happy, passionate and productive business owners making a very good living from the products they promote.

I wouldn't be here if that wasn't the case.

What's more, the nature of the business means that you as a business owner aren't just looking to move huge volumes—that's not the point at all. We all do a bit of selling and a bit of business building and then, as a result of the business model and money saved on fixed rate marketing, we all enjoy the benefit of cashing in on the commission that would have been spent on those business costs.

It's disruption at its best, and it's the future of quality products sold by honest, trustworthy business owners taking responsibility for their income, creating a side hustle and building an empire. I kid you not, this really is the future.

If this business model interests you and you want to be part of a revolutionary way to create wealth, with opportunities as vast as your imagination, then please get in touch.

Going back to one of our earlier chapters, don't shrink your dream circle to fit your income circle—do it the right way. Expand your income and live the life you've always wanted.

I am here and waiting to help you do exactly that and I can't wait to meet you.

Key Takeaways

- Starting a business from scratch is impossibly complex. There's no need to stress yourself out with that idea.

- 95% of the core business services have already been created, honed and made available to you from day one.

- You don't need to be a salesperson; you need to be passionate and vocal.

- When you have a small base of customers, you create a team of other sellers and they create exponential growth for you to earn from, as they do from their teams.

If this book has resonated with you, and you'd like to explore the possibilities of having your own home-based business to experience entrepreneurial freedom for yourself, then visit www.CliffWalker.com/Consultation to schedule a Complimentary Home-Based Business Assessment Consultation (Value £375.00).

NOTES

NOTES

NOTES

NOTES

THE ENTREPRENEUR MINDSET SHIFT

Owning Your Own Global Home Business

NOTES

NOTES

NOTES

NOTES